Neil Mac

Taking the Hell out of Homework

A manual for parents and home educators

SEN Marketing

www.senbooks.co.uk

COPYRIGHT STATEMENT

Copyright © Neil MacKay 2010

SEN Marketing
618 Leeds Road, Outwood
Wakefield
West Yorkshire, WF1 2LT
United Kingdom
Tel/FAX: +44 (0) 1924 871697
www.senbooks.co.uk

ISBN: 978 1903842 09 6

First published: January 2011

Printed and bound in the UK by J F Print Ltd., Sparkford

Taking the Hell out of Homework

Contents

Section 1 – Strategies and approaches

Section 2 – Materials and practice activities

Acknowledgements

I am very grateful to the schools, local authorities and dyslexia associations listed below for giving me the opportunity to work with parents and children. Also I would like to thank the parents and children for giving me permission to use their photographs to illustrate the various ideas and activities.

- Dyslexia Association of Hong Kong
- Dyslexia Foundation of New Zealand (4D)
- Hafren Primary School, Newtown Powys
- Hawarden High School, Flintshire
- Kesteven and Sleaford High School, Lincolnshire
- King's School, Ely
- Mab Lane Primary School, Liverpool
- Orkney Education Service
- Preston and District Dyslexia Association (PADDA)
- Rhosnesni Cluster, Wrexham
- Walsall Wood Primary School, Walsall
- Welsh Dyslexia Project

A very special vote of thanks is due to June Todd, Head Teacher of Mab Lane Primary School in Liverpool for her confidence in the initial vision and her continued support in providing facilities for a number of parent and child workshops and also to the West Derby Learning Network for providing funding.

Finally, my wife has been an invaluable sounding board for ideas and she has also kept me grounded during some flights of fancy – thank you, Carole.

On Children
Kahlil Gibran

Your children are not your children.
They are the sons and daughters of Life's
   longing for itself.
They come through you but not from you,
and though they are with you yet they belong
   not to you.

You may give them your love but not your
   thoughts,
for they have their own thoughts.
You may house their bodies but not their
   souls,
for their souls dwell in the house of tomorrow,
which you cannot visit, not even in your
   dreams.
You may strive to be like them,
but seek not to make them like you.
For life goes not backward nor tarries with
   yesterday.

You are the bows from which your children,
   as living arrows, are sent forth.
The archer sees the mark upon the path of the
   infinite,
and He bends you with His might
that His arrows may go swift and far.
Let your bending in the archer's hand be for
   gladness;
For even as He loves the arrow that flies,
so He loves also the bow that is stable.

Section 1 – Strategies and Approaches

Working with your child at home

Being a parent is stressful at the best of times – and never more so than when helping a child with homework tasks. And if the child has learning needs the potential for stress can be much greater and there is always the risk of 'tears before bedtime'!

A child's fear of failure and the emotional baggage carried by parents can get in the way of effective working together. Perhaps one of the greatest gifts we can give our children is the realisation that it is ok to find some things difficult. Put it another way – we love you as you are!

Having said all this, the situation will always arise when a child needs help and a parent does not know quite how to go about it. The focus of this book is to give parents some of the 'tricks of the trade'. Also I hope that you will develop the confidence to work at home with techniques you know to be appropriate and successful.

Homework is a curse for many parents/carers as well as for our children. As the father of a child with additional learning needs, nothing, absolutely nothing has caused more conflict and grief than homework and, when I rule the world, it will be banned! The problem is that a typical, undifferentiated piece of homework (undifferentiated in this context means something which is given to the whole class without much thought about how difficult some might find it) will take some children a few minutes and some a few hours. In the case of one of my own children, three notional '20 minute homeworks' could take her over three hours and, because she is a very conscientious student, she would put the time in to the exclusion of all else, especially having any form of a life.

So this book is written for Corinne, and children across the world (and their parents) who are victims of homework.

The right to learn differently

'stress free is error free'

It is suggested that up to 80% of difficulties associated with learning new ideas and skills are due to stress. When I run training courses for parents and children I always make a point of asking parents to refrain from ever saying to their child "You are doing it wrong". What this usually means is "You are not doing it the way I would". A key principle of effective 'parenting for homework' is to accept that 'our children are not us' and to support them to learn and work in the ways that suit their unique blend of talents and preferences.

This can require a paradigm shift for some adults. When parents share their concerns about a child's progress I always stop them and ask them to begin by identifying their child's strengths; sadly many parents find this hard to do at first — they have focussed for so long on the 'can'ts' that it becomes almost impossible for them to see their child in a positive light.

So stop, just for a minute, and think about all the things that your child does that you value and appreciate – why not jot them down? Is s/he caring, responsible, reliable, sensitive, creative, enthusiastic? These 'soft skills' are recognised as being increasingly important in employment.

It helps also to identify your child's preferred ways of working so that you can set them up to succeed. This is often a complete turnaround from the way we ourselves were taught. For many of us teaching was based around the principle that mindless repetition was the key to learning, so when, for example, we struggled to spell words we had to write them out 10 times. This approach is completely useless, has never worked and yet is still seen by many as an important strategy. Giving children more and more of what they cannot do in order to get better at it flies in the face of reason, to say nothing of the psychology of learning! It is important that we parents resist the temptation to impose the comfortable but ineffective practices of our own schooling on our children.

How does your child prefer to learn?

In over 30 years of teaching I have never met a child who does not want to learn, although I have met many who have all but given up because of the struggle of being expected to learn in uncomfortable or impossible ways. Interestingly, once these children have discovered their unique learning patterns and have been given permission to learn differently, most go on to learn very effectively. Some take longer than others to move on and the time it takes seems to depend on the amount of baggage being carried around from previous failures and battles with an inflexible system.

Finding out how your child prefers to think and learn can be an illuminating experience and my preferred method is to use a mind map (see overleaf). This exercise helps us find out the different ways that our children are smart.

Using the mind map on the next page work with your child and ask them to:

1. Colour each of the 'triangles' closest to the centre of the map – Music, Picture etc

2. Take a heading and ask your child to highlight and/or underline any statement that 'sounds like me'. This is often best done if the parent reads the descriptor and the child decides. If in doubt please go with the child's opinion. This mind map is only intended to be a snapshot in time and many preferences change as they grow in confidence and experience. It may help to view these preferences as your child's 'comfort zone'. This zone may initially be quite narrow but it will expand as baggage from previous failure is cast off. Even if the parent is found to be right in the future, giving the child the right to choose is an important message at this stage of building a working relationship.

With a colour pen mark everything that describes YOU.

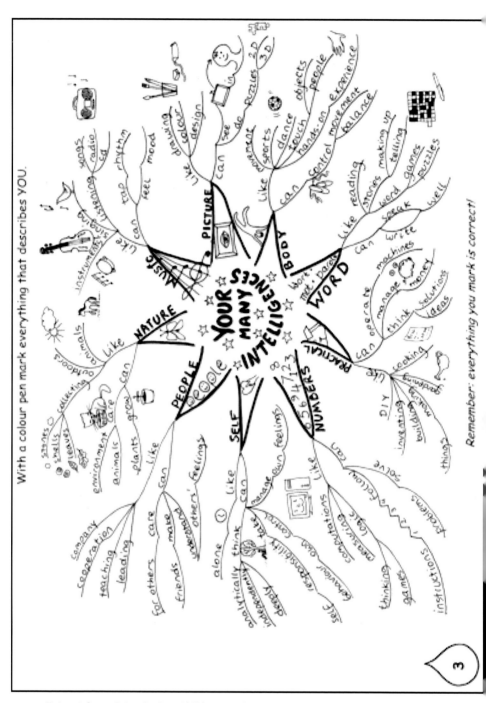

Remember: everything you mark is correct!

Extract from *Introducing Children to their Intelligences* by Eva Hoffman.
Published by Learn to Learn, © 2001.

3. Work around the map for your child to underline and/or highlight personal preferences. It is quite likely that in one or two areas s/he will have little or no preferences, which is quite normal – for example I do not register any preferences in the 'picture' strand because I am definitely not a picture person.

4. Work with your child to choose three main headings to represent a 'core learning strategy'. This strategy will form the basis for most learning in the future and is where your child currently feels most comfortable. In my case, I am most comfortable using activities involving Word, Body and People.

When you have finished it will look something like this:

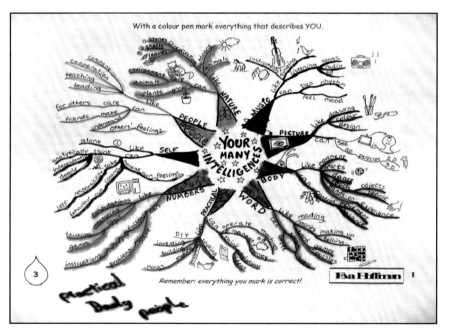

Based on an extract from *Introducing Children to their Intelligences* by Eva Hoffman. Published by Learn to Learn, © 2001.

Below is a short explanation of how each preference may be applied to learning.

LEARNING THE WAY YOU LEARN BEST

Multiple Learning Preferences

Did you know that:

- there are at least 7 preferences and each has its own best way of learning – ways to 'work smart'?

- we all possess varying degrees and levels of these intelligences?

- successful learners use a range of methods and select them to suit the learning tasks in hand?

I suggest you and your child discuss the information below and choose some ways to learn based on them.

1. 'Body Smart'

- Often well coordinated

- Often good at sport

- **Learns best by** doing, hands on, working on the move

2. 'Word Smart'

- Good at reading, writing and speaking

- Likes humour, jokes

- **Learns best by** saying out loud, explaining, repeating

3. 'Number Smart'

- Likes numbers, solving problems etc

- Good at interpreting data, sorting things out

- **Learns best by** looking for patterns, arranging information in order

4. 'Art Smart'

- Good at visualizing and `seeing' in the mind's eye
- Thinking in pictures
- **Learns best through** colour, mind maps, visual presentation of information

5. 'Music Smart'

- Has a feel for rhythm, melody, pitch
- Likes background music
- **Learns best through** rhythm, rhyme, melody, songs, rapping

6. 'People Smart'

- Sensitive – often good listeners/mediators
- Tuned into the feelings of others
- **Learns best through** working with others, cooperative learning, teaching others

7. 'Self Smart'

- Knows themselves well
- Prefers to work alone – independent
- **Learns best through** working at own pace, on individual projects

Please make a note of your child's 3 main learning preferences – I will come back to this shortly.

Preference 1 ....

Preference 2 ....

Preference 3 ....

These three preferences can be used to develop your **Core Learning Strategy** – the combination of techniques that work for most learning tasks.

This table shows how to turn core learning strategies into action. Once you have identified your child's preferences then add them to the Core Learning Strategy boxes on page 18.

Explore the subject

Seven ways to explore a subject in depth	
1. **Put it in your own words - explain to a friend**	You can only be effective if you really understand and can communicate that understanding.
2. **Make a mind map**	Best if some or all of the information is on post-its or strips of paper, (more information will follow on this technique). Explain it to a friend to involve auditory, linguistic and interpersonal preferences; use colour and drawings to lock in the visual element – this will help in the exam room.
3. **Discuss it or just say it out loud**	Make a recording of someone reading the passage aloud for listening to on a tape player or mp3 device. If you need the visual, too use a web-cam. The power of hearing your own voice is well-known in education.

4. List main points in a logical order	Writing information on strips of paper and organising them to form a flow chart or mind map. Explaining the logic behind the chosen order brings other styles into play.
5. Do something physical – either with the information or while working on it	Moving helps! Just walking around the room while repeating information out loud can work. Tapping in time as you chant information can be effective as can learning while on an exercise machine – try using a music stand.
6. Decide how it fits in with existing knowledge	Listing what you already know is good. Deliberately link new knowledge to old, through pictures, word association, visualisation, etc. Mind maps are particularly effective, as is working with a friend. Try listing and matching information on strips of paper.
7. Write a song, jingle or rap to summarise your learning	Most of us seem to know the words to dozens of songs without ever consciously setting out to learn them. Using rhythm and rhyme as a learning aid can be very effective.

The final stage is to link preferences with techniques, using the table below. It may be that your child prefers to work in a way which is not listed above – my advice is to go with it, perhaps with a challenge to prove that it works. If it does, then all is well, if it does not then this needs to be acknowledged gently and an alternative strategy put in place.

I think it was Einstein who said something like, "It's called research because we do not know the answer", the journey of exploring, confirming and rejecting learning preferences, is vitally important as it forms the bedrock of future learning and also establishes the emotional climate for subsequent work together.

This 'Core Learning Strategy' table is repeated on page 87 and can be copied and completed to guide future learning.

Core Learning Strategy

Learning Preference	Learning Technique
1.	
2.	
3.	

Each time I learn I will make sure I:

1. ....

2. ....

3. ....

18

Once again illustrating from personal experience, as a 'body, word and people' learner I find I learn best when I:

1. Put information on post-it notes so I can touch it and move it around into patterns that suit me.

2. Say out loud what I am doing – it especially helps me to put information into my own words rather than just copying from a page or screen.

3. Explain what I am trying to do to other people – possibly teaching them even if they already know how to do it.

When I do these three things as my core learning strategy I can almost guarantee the success of my learning; the challenge is to develop a preferred core with your child.

Putting knowledge into practice

At this point you should be fairly clear about your child's current learning preferences, but bear in mind that these may well change in the future. The next step is to explore these preferences and prove to your child that working differently really works.

The activities below are intended as a fun way of exploring learning preferences and building success. I use them as part of my 'Parent and Child' workshops and they are always successful, as long as parents take a step back and allow the children to explore the process for themselves.

Health warning - allowing parental ego to become linked with a child's performance in the coming activities is a recipe for disaster!

The Task:

Activity Time

- You have 5 minutes to use a combination (at least 2!) of your preferred learning methods to learn a shopping list which follows.
  (Please don't just read it through!)

- When the time is up you will be asked to write the list from memory.

Set a Target score   (?/18)

THE SHOPPING LIST

- Sausages
- Toothpaste
- Flour
- Washing-up Liquid
- Carrots
- Cheese
- Shampoo
- Fish fingers
- Onions

- Phone card
- Bread
- Potatoes
- Milk
- Lemonade
- Baked beans
- Dog food
- Tomato soup
- Pizza

Target Score /18
Actual Score /18

The trick is to apply your child's core learning strategy to the shopping list and to explore ways of making learning effective. Regardless of core learning strategy, most brains seem to prefer some sort of order and structure when it comes to learning. Order and structure is another ways of saying "look for ways to organise the information into bite sized chunks".

To learn any information effectively it is necessary to come up with an overall method and a chunking strategy, both based around your child's comfort zone. Later I will show how to turn text into 'learnable lists' but for now the shopping list will do the trick.

Learning to remember

Initially we need a 'big picture plan' to organise the information, the final choice of plan being determined by your child's preferences. The following approaches have proved successful in the past:

Learning Preference	Learning Strategy
Picture	• Mental journey around supermarket – see yourself putting items into trolley • Mental journey around kitchen – see yourself putting items in cupboards • Mind map/concept web • Draw items (paper plates work well to create bizarre menus).
Body/practical	• As for picture – try to feel yourself in action. • Mime placing objects into the cupboards and say the names of items as you do it • Write the name of each item on a separate piece of paper • Cluster them according to your criteria • Walk about the room while learning
Number	• Look for logical links between items (vegetables, liquids etc.) organise accordingly • Alphabetical order • Write name of each item on a separate piece of paper. • Cluster them according to your criteria

Or you could consider:

Learning Preference	Learning Strategy
Emotional	• Create funny or strange menu combinations – have fun with the task • Link 'forgotten' items with things you remembered easily, try a 'funny' or unusual link

Word	• Cluster items:
	  i) say out loud with rhythm and rhyme
	  ii) break into clusters of 4-5 items, repeat lists out loud
	• Look for mnemonic opportunities

People	• Work with a partner • Ask someone to test you
Self	• Work on your own • Plan your own way to learn and test yourself
Nature	• Link to things or sounds in nature • Group items for your guinea pig
Music	• Group items to say with rhythm • Shopping list rap?

Spend time discussing ideas with your child and try to have fun with crazy ideas. While you are exploring possibilities write each item down on a separate post-it note – the smaller ones are best (say 50mm x 50mm). This will allow your child to touch and manipulate the information, something which seems to lock the learning, regardless of any other learning preferences.

Let us consider some possibilities:

Child 1: is currently a picture, body, music preferred learner with a quirky sense of humour.

Picture learners are often able to visualise and hold vivid pictures in their head. Touching the learning in the form of post-it notes also helps to build and maintain the picture and the sense of humour may add an important emotional hook. One organisational strategy could be:

1. Drawing a plan of the kitchen (picture smart)

2. Sticking post-it notes on the appropriate cupboards, on the fridge, freezer, pantry etc. (body smart)

3. Make a list of the cupboards and places in which everything has been placed as the organisational strategy (number smart) (learning strategy to follow)
    - Under sink
    - Fridge
    - Over cooker, etc.

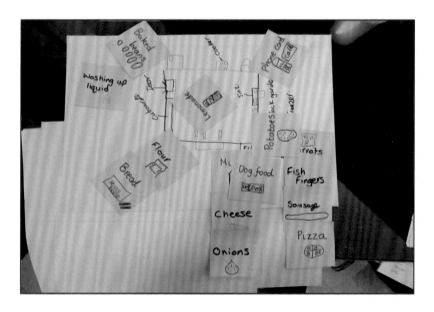

Another strategy could be to:

1. Create some crazy menus – perhaps with an appropriate theme (picture/emotional)

2. Draw plates and illustrate with pictures of the items on the plates (picture)

3. Use the post-it notes to label the items (body)

4. Give each menu/plate a suitable name (picture/emotional)

Plates of food

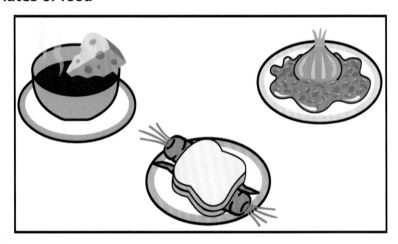

Child 2: is currently a number and word preferred learner who also has strong 'self' tendencies.

Number learners like order and sequence and may prefer to sort the items into alphabetical order, food groups or another appropriate approach. Word learners also enjoy opportunities to explain what they are doing and teach others. One preferred strategy could be:

1. Go for alphabetical order or 'food groups'
2. Head up a large sheet of paper with A, B, C or Veg, Liquids, etc.
3. Stick post-it notes under appropriate headings
4. Make a list of the chosen headings
5. Explain this system to parent

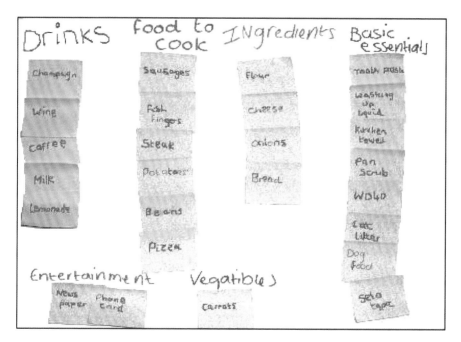

A word to the wise – there are often one or two items that do not easily fit a pattern. In this case a heading like 'Stuff' can be very useful, as long as it does not include too many items.

Organising to remember

The children appear to have 18 items to learn. However they have already organised the items under headings and often just learning the headings – what Tony Buzan would call the 'basic ordering ideas' – can trigger the rest of the information. So, rather than try to learn all 18 items, it is helpful to develop a preferred strategy to remember the basic ordering ideas, on the grounds that it is easier to learn 5 or 6 headings than 18 separate items. (See Stage 2 (page 91) for strategies for learning headings).

> **Time spent learning the main headings really pays off**

Being a body/music learner Child 1 might enjoy having the headings on separate post-it notes and singing, clapping or rapping them while placing them on the table, then doing the same with the items in each sub-list.

Alternatively a body/picture learner may prefer to go on a mental journey around the kitchen and recite the list of items placed in each cupboard. Parents can help by chanting "What's in the fridge, what's under the sink", etc. This will also work with the funny menus.

Child 2 has already created order within the list by working alphabetically and also needs to learn the basic ordering ideas in preferred ways. A version of "What's in the 'A's, what's in the 'B's" will work and, being a word/people learner child 2 may find that explaining the process or teaching it to someone else helps. Just saying it out loud with rhythm can also be very effective.

The shopping list quiz

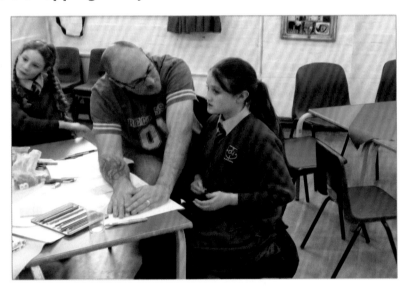

Shortly, it will be time to see if the techniques are effective by challenging your child to get a target score – I suggest you push for around half marks but never, ever 18/18 because any test that demands full marks is unrealistic and unfair. This will also give an opportunity for parents to support the setting of realistic and achievable targets and to emphasise that there is no failure, only feedback. To put it another way, mistakes mean that someone is really trying.

If your child digs in for a low score, please recognise it as a sign of a 'baggage driven' lack of confidence; accept playing safe for now in the certain knowledge that next time increased confidence will permit a more realistic target. Parents can help by offering to write down the items as the child dictates and also by giving reminders of the basic ordering ideas.

When I do this in workshop settings it is very unusual for any child not to equal or beat their target score and, in many cases, they remember all of the items, to the amazement and joy of their parents. The reasons for this success are many: the activity was a challenge with nothing at stake – apart from a gentle teasing with "I bet you can't get that score"; the learning was done in personalised and preferred ways; the task was actually quite enjoyable; it was done in a very multisensory way, using a wide range of senses, touch, vision, hearing, etc. which is also a cornerstone of effective learning; and finally the task was broken down into basic ordering ideas and more manageable chunks. All of which helps to 'lock the learning'.

Personalising the learning process

Below are some personalised strategies, each worked well for the individuals concerned because they did it their way.

The 'mental journey around a supermarket' approach

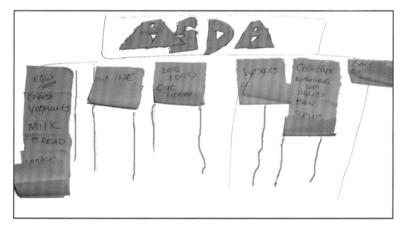

The 'super organised/control freak' approach

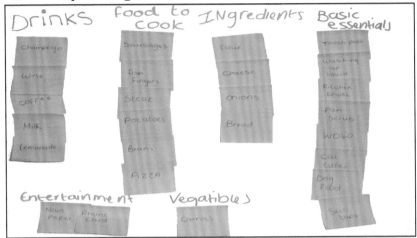

The 'my way or the highway' approach

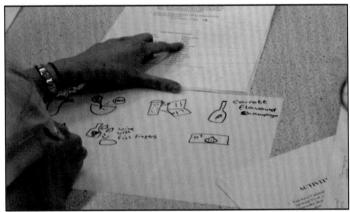

The 'take a walk around my kitchen' approach

The 'hieroglyphics are cool' approach

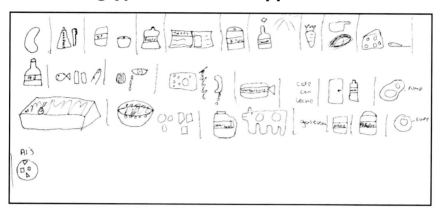

A word to the wise - each approach is good if it works, if it does not work then it needs changing. It really is as simple as that!

Learning basic ordering ideas

I have already mentioned chanting and rapping, both of which are often more effective if linked to movement, in fact these techniques can be surprisingly effective!
A visual journey or actually visualising a picture or a plan of the kitchen or the aisles in your local supermarket can also be effective as preferred ways of learning. Let us suppose that the plan for organising the shopping list is the creation of five or six bizarre menus for aliens, each alien having a suitably memorable name which ideally reflects the choice of items on the menu. So Alien Yuk might have a phone card pizza with extra dog food, washed down with.......etc.

When the ideas can be learnt in any order, it can be effective for your child to create a series of short stories within each basic ordering idea.

Vegetable cupboard story

"One night the onions were crying because they couldn't find their phone card in the dark. The carrots agreed to help them" ...... and so on.

I know that phone cards are not usually kept with vegetables but this seemed like an opportunity to work in an item which otherwise may have ended up under 'stuff'. Once the mini story is completed it must be illustrated with a quick picture. This picture is essential as it forces the brain to transform the words into a picture, effectively moving the information from one side of the brain to the other. Some children will see a picture in their mind before they think of a story, in which case encourage them to draw the picture first, basically support them to do whatever comes naturally.

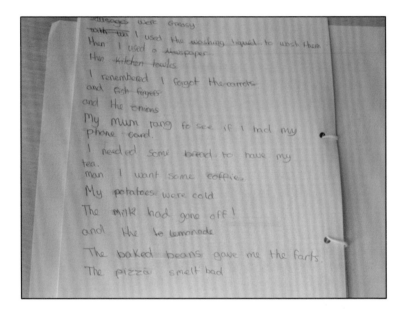

See Stage 2 for another learning challenge for you to practice the techniques – The 'Police Kit List' Challenge.

The proof is in the pudding: meeting/beating the target score

Now is the time to set the quiz challenge and see if your child can equal or maybe even beat the target. I strongly suggest you offer gentle help and support to ensure success, especially if past failures are colouring attitudes to learning. Not only is it very unusual for children not to meet their targets, but many are still successful an hour, a day and a week later – in other words, personalising learning in this way secures long term gains because the information has moved from the short term memory to the long term memory.

Doing it for real

I suggest you use the 'police kit list' activity on page 89 to reinforce the technique. See how little guidance you can give while always looking over their shoulders to make sure the process is being done optimally. Children being children will often quickly revert to old habits, even though these habits do not work. So it is important to ensure that this efficient and personalised process is applied whenever possible.

The next challenge

You and your child have found a good way to learn lists. Unfortunately few learning tasks come pre-packaged in the form of 'learnable lists'. Happily though, turning paragraphs and pages of information into learnable lists is not only quite straightforward, but the process itself also helps to lock the learning in the long term memory. The key is 'paired reading'.

The power of paired reading

When I first read with my own children, obviously as a Dad rather than as a teacher, I would read them stories. Then, as they got older, we would share the reading, perhaps reading a page each. This was fine until my youngest daughter began to experience difficulties. At this point the shared reading process became a source of frustration and she began to lose enjoyment in reading. Then I found out about paired reading. It changed our reading relationship and almost every parent who has tried it says the same.

A common comment from parents of older children in particular (9 & 10 upwards into teens) is that since we have been using paired reading we are reading together easily and happily, just like we used to.

Why bother to read?

Before we go any further, it may be helpful to reflect on the way reading is taught and how that teaching process can cause problems for children who have become reluctant readers.

When adults choose to read, it is on our terms, it is usually our choice of material and we have a very clear reason for engaging in the reading process, maybe for pleasure, research, general interest etc. However, many reluctant readers are given a book to read because it will be 'good for them' and be expected to 'read for pleasure', because that is apparently good for them too! Also there may be a perception, often parent driven and picked up by the child, that books that are 'too easy' are to be discouraged. Now this is just plain wrong if the purpose of reading is for pleasure.

As someone who is addicted to reading I choose my books carefully for whatever purpose I have in mind at the time, in other words I read to fulfil certain needs. If the need is for relaxation, perhaps during a long haul flight, I will choose an easy read – page turner preferred. I will also carry something which requires more concentration in case I feel the need for more stimulation. The point is I read for a purpose and vary the material accordingly.
I strongly believe children deserve the same control over what they read.

Now I can already hear the thinking: "If I give my child the choice s/he won't read anything". If this is the case, it is probably because, for your child at this particular moment in time, the reading 'wiifme' factor (what's in it for me) is far too low; the reading process is slow, boring and, above all else, perceived as pointless. Paired reading takes children back to when reading was easy, relaxed and, above all else, purposeful.

The principles of paired reading

Principle 1:

Instead of parent and child sharing the reading – "You read then I'll read" – both read out loud at the same time. This may sound strange but it is simply the best and most painless way I know of improving comprehension, fluency and accuracy.

Principle 2:

It must be your child's choice of reading material, whatever they want to read is alright. This is to remove the baggage of years of being told which tedious book from the reading scheme to read next and to begin to establish reading as a purposeful activity. In fact I think the ability and willingness to read effectively for a purpose is much more important than reading for pleasure. Who am I to tell anyone, child or adult, what they *should* find pleasurable?

Principle 3:

Anything with printed words will do, so long as your child wants or needs to read it. So the manual for a new mobile phone or piece of software is fine, as is the TV page, sports or fashion or even the 'who kissed who' articles in newspapers. Too simple is much better than too hard, though paired reading also works really well at the outer limits of easy reading. The formula is simple:

Child + printed words + 'need to read' + supportive, non judgemental parent = effective paired reading

Principle 4:

Parent and child sit side by side and both read out loud together, with the parent pointing at the words as they are read. If the child struggles with a word or 'refuses' the adult just reads on – no comment, no teaching, just slowing down slightly and carrying on, pointing at the words until the child climbs back onto the sentence, and s/he will.

Principle 5:

Relax and enjoy!

Some tricks of the trade:

Parents please:

a. "Tell the story with your voice", the more expression the better, as this aids comprehension. Later encourage your child to do the same. The ability to read with expression depends on comprehension and failure to do so suggest that your child is 'barking at print,' i.e. reading the words but not really understanding the message.

b. As your child begins to read with fluency, try saying the next word very slightly after your child. This places responsibility for cuing the word on your child and helps develop reading. Be ready to read normally the minute a problem occurs.

c. Never, ever ask your child to practice a problem word or be in any way critical. Enjoyment = stress free!

Paired reading and a typical homework task

A typical homework task will often be a comprehension passage with questions to answer. The question is "What is the best thing to do first?"

Advice for doing comprehensions

- Do we say:
- "Read the passage all the way through before you start"?

Traditionally, children have been told to read the passage all the way through before starting. This is wrong!

Some slower readers spend so long battling through the text that they never get to the questions, or they run out of time and are rarely able to get to the 'high tariff' questions which carry the most marks.

Another suggestion could be to read the questions first. This is better but still wrong!

Advice for doing comprehensions

- Do we say:
- "Read the questions before you start"?

Reading the questions first is better than starting with the passage, but there is an even better way to approach comprehension tasks:

It works like this:

Stages	Focus	**Questions to Ask**	**Rationale**
Stage 1	Title	• What does the title mean? • What is this about? • What do I know already? • Where does it fit in with other work? • What have I got to do?	The title often suggests a series of informed guesses regarding likely content, direction and requirements. It is also the basis for 'contextual guessing'* when unfamiliar words are presented.
Stage 2	Captions and Pictures	To be processed together. In particular scan and examine: • Anything in bold • Anything in a box • Anything with an arrow or line • Any pictures, diagrams or charts • Any foot notes • Any words that leap out of the text	Captions and pictures continue the process of contextual guessing. This is a particularly important skill for dyslexic learners who tend to think faster than they read. Some of the text will naturally catch the eye. When it does, read it.

***Contextual guessing** takes place when a child uses context to make a decision about how to read an unfamiliar word.

		Questions to ask	**Rationale**
<u>Stage 3</u>	Questions	Pair read all the ***questions*** through before starting. Then ask yourself: • What does the question mean - can I paraphrase it? • How much do I need to write – link to the marking value if appropriate? • Have I already found the answer through captions and pictures? • Do I have a rough idea of where the answer might be in the text? • Do any of the later questions provide answers for earlier ones? (They often do!) • **Key Question** - How many questions can you answer before reading the text?	Three important 'Work smart rather than hard' principles need to be understood: 1. Many questions can and should be answered without a thorough reading of text 2. 'Free gift' answers are often available within the body of the text or later questions 3. 'If in doubt, leave it out'. Question-spot for the easy ones first, then go back when you have finished
<u>Stage 4</u>	Read	• Read the passage	Opportunity here to look at answers and confirm, modify or change as appropriate

See Stage 2 for a worked example, page 94.

This activity needs to be practised many times with a variety of comprehensions in a range of subjects. However, once it becomes 'custom and practice' it can become a life skill which saves hours of wading through material only to find out that it is not relevant. It is also a great technique to use in exams, especially when under pressure of time. An added bonus is a general improvement in reading efficiency.

The TCP-QR process also empowers your child to make intelligent and informed guesses at unfamiliar words because s/he already knows so much about the passage. Sometimes it will be necessary to miss out a word and read to the full stop in order to make the guess. But in almost every case the guess will be guided by TCP-QR and be contextually appropriate. For example, contextually appropriate could mean reading the word "ships" as "boats" – they are not quite the same, but either word will probably do in terms of carrying the meaning of the sentence.

TCP-QR + Paired Reading – the strategy for children who think faster than they read

The most efficient technique is:

1. Do TCP-Q first. If there are no questions, just work with your child to discuss TCP.

2. See if any questions can be answered before reading the passage – parents please write down any answers, even if they are possibly wrong. TCP is not an exact science and it is important to establish the principle of making educated guesses which later require modification in the light of new evidence. Note: Transcribing wrong answers can provide valuable opportunities for discussion.

3. Pair read the passage, challenging your child to stop when answers to questions are found in the text or where guesses need to be modified.

4. If your child does not seem to be picking up any answers try:

> i) Stopping after an 'obvious answer' and see if your child can spot it.

> ii) Pair reading the passage all the way through and then working through the questions one by one.

Often you will be amazed at the amount of detail that has been picked up.

5. Pair read the questions again and record your child's responses.

6. Finally pair read each question and its answer and check that your child is happy with the answer.

A word to the wise – I strongly advise you not to make your child copy out the answers that you have already recorded - what a waste of time! Instead inform your school that, from time to time, your child will hand in work that has been dictated to you. This could be in your hand or typed in, either way all you are doing is being the scribe and making a fair copy of your child's answers. Few good schools will have a problem with this approach and many will be delighted to support you.

However, it is essential that parents play fair and record faithfully what is said, even if, maybe especially if, the answers are wrong or could be improved. Once schools realise that you are only making a true copy, any resistance usually fades. Failure to play fair runs the risk of end of year reports with phrases like "John is forging his way steadily ahead"!

Paired reading and learning for tests

Earlier the shopping list activity demonstrated that learning lists is not a problem, provided it is done in preferred ways.   Unfortunately the information needed to learn for tests rarely comes pre-packaged in list form. Paired reading is the basis of an easy way to process information into lists for learning, especially when combined with TCP-QR.

Consider the passage below; instead of asking questions in the form of a traditional comprehension task, this activity requires the reader to identify information related to four themes:

- When
- Where
- Characters
- Events

From paired reading to 'learnable lists'

1. Before pair reading, ask your child to highlight each of the theme words (when, where, characters, events) in a different colour.

2. Pair read, asking your child to stop reading whenever s/he comes across information which relates to when, where, characters or events. You may need to help by stopping reading yourself and share what you have found.

3. Decide on the theme that has been identified and highlight the information in the appropriate colour.

Draw a picture of what the story is about in the middle of a blank page.
On thick branches write such words as: WHEN (time of action),
WHERE (place of action),
CHARACTERS (names of people/animals),
EVENTS (most important things that happened).

If you want, you may add branches with such words as THEME and 'OPINION.
On thin branches write details connected with the key words.

"JACK'S NEW AEROPLANE"

Jack and Richard were cousins. They were also very good friends and they liked playing together.
One day, in the middle of summer, Jack came to Richard and brought with him his new toy, a remote controlled aeroplane! It was quite big, painted with silver paint and had some red pictures on the tail.
The boys were very excited and decided to go to the garden to fly the plane straight away.
They had a lot of fun. The plane was fantastic! It flew quite high and made some funny noises when landing.
It was Richard's turn to fly the plane. In his excitement he pressed a button on the remote control very hard and the plane flew high, very high, and landed on the top of a tree! Richard found a long stick and tried to get the plane down. But the stick was not long enough. Then Jack thought of something else: he started shaking the tree hard, very hard, and in the end the plane fell to the ground with a big bang.
Jack picked up the plane, and Richard ... picked up a broken wing... Oh dear!...
Both boys were very upset and very angry at the same time. Jack blamed Richard for flying the plane too high, and Richard blamed Jack for shaking the tree too hard...
In the end they both agreed that getting angry and blaming each other was not going to help.
They took the plane and its broken wing, and went home to find some glue.

Remember: everything you write or draw is correct!   Have fun!

Extract from *Introducing Children to Mind Mapping* by Eva Hoffman.
Published by Learn to Learn, © 2001.

When you have finished it could look something like this:

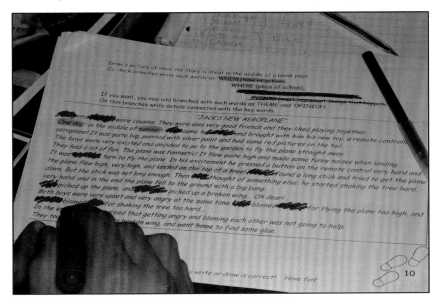

Extract from *Introducing Children to Mind Mapping* by Eva Hoffman.
Published by Learn to Learn, © 2001.

Then:

- Get some small post-it notes
- Parents write each piece of highlighted information on a separate post-it note and stick on the table

Alternatively, some children prefer to work straight from the highlighted passage.

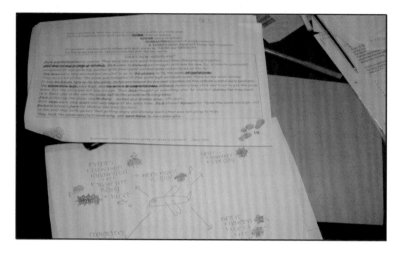

- Ask your child to choose a preferred way to organise the post-its under the theme headings. Below are examples of organising via a flow chart or mind map, but these are no more than suggestions. The preferred method of organisation is only wrong if it does not work for your child.

Below are more personalised approaches – each worked well for the individual concerned.

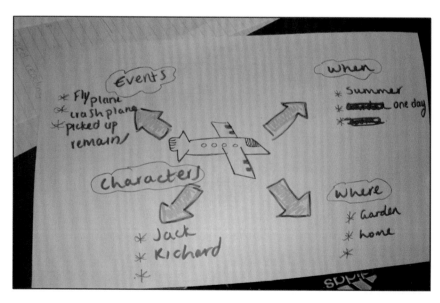

44

To get this plan I said:

- Draw a picture in the centre of the page that represents something from the story
- Write the four themes around the picture
- Put the highlighted information from the passage on to the page in any way you like

Note: If the highlighted information is written on post-it notes it allows the child to do the thinking without having to worry about the writing.

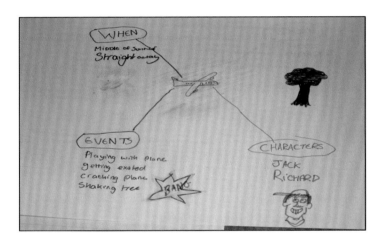

A word to the wise – try to keep quiet if you see your child heading up a blind alley. Be supportive, non-judgemental and use the opportunity to discuss more effective approaches next time. Be warned that some seemingly bizarre preferred approaches may actually work! In this situation the mantra is:

"A closed mouth gathers no feet."

The next two maps are made using 'Kidspiration':

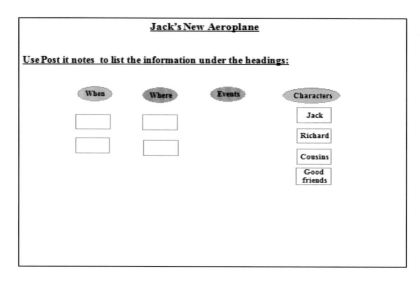

(You can buy a copy of the software program from www.senbooks.co.uk if you like this idea.)

A flow chart or mind map could be a preferred way of organising the information, or any other way that works for your child. Whichever way is preferred, challenge your child to build up the chart or map using the post-it notes.

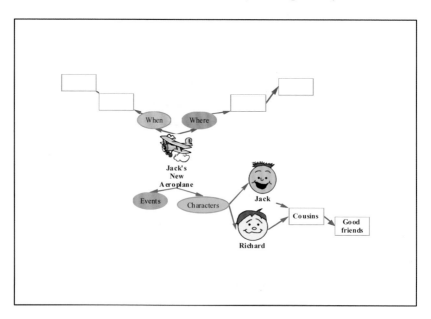

The map below is made using `Inspiration'. For a free trial download go to www.inspiration.com.

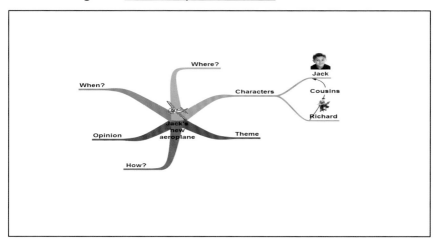

Now it is a case of using the core learning strategies identified earlier to:

1. Learn the four themes (basic ordering ideas) using techniques from the shopping list activity.

2. Learn the information which goes with each theme using preferred strategies.

Also, try taking off all the post-it notes and challenging your child to:

1. Re-build the flow chart or mind map.

2. Reorganise the information into another form - from mind map to flow chart etc.

Finally, ask your child some questions about the passage.

For example:

1. How were Jack and Richard related?

2. At what time of the year did this all take place?

3. Give me some detail about Jack's new toy.

4. What did the plane do when it landed?

I think you will be amazed at the level of recall and the amount of detail remembered.

This technique is generally very successful but it needs to be taught with patience, respect and tolerance for personalised approaches which may be very different from ours. Also please be aware that 'taught is not learnt' and any new skill needs to be practiced and re-visited at least ten to twenty times before it even begins to become automatic.

See page 88 for another practice activity.

Revising for tests and exams

Many of the techniques mentioned so far were originally developed to support dyslexic students when revising for GCSE and A level exams. Then they were modified for use across a range of learning issues. The basic principle introduced through the shopping list test, of creating learnable lists and then producing them in different, personalised forms, also applies to revision for public exams. Below are some examples of how students have applied their individual learning preferences to personalise their lists in ways which are unique, memorable and quick to reproduce in the exam room as an aide memoire before answering a question.

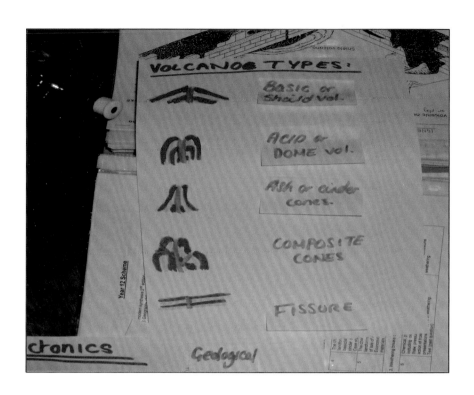

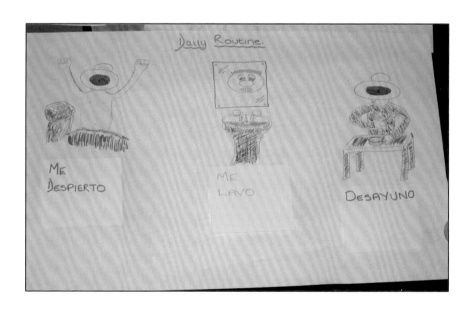

49

Spelling

The pressures placed on parents by the demands of the weekly spelling test are well known, though often underestimated by schools and teachers. Learning 10 spellings can take all week, only to find that the words are forgotten as soon as the test is over. In other words the learning that has taken place has gone into the 'state related memory' meaning that the learnt words are only available during the test situation rather than during any form of normal writing.

There are a number of reasons for this lack of transfer between learning spellings for tests and for use in writing. This is mainly due to the use of learning strategies which are ineffective, inefficient and often based on the way we were taught.

For example, one traditional approach is to write each word down a notional 10 times – and then again and again. For all but a few children this 'correction based' approach is worse than useless: it does not work and it never has. However it can be comforting to us because we feel we are at least doing something to help. Another inefficient though very popular strategy used in schools and often recommended to parents is 'Look, Cover, Write, Check'. Whilst it is popular it is arguably of limited value, and more effective strategies are shown below.

Personalising the spelling process

Your child will already have a core learning strategy developed through earlier activities. Now it is time to apply this core to the learning of spellings. But before we can start we do need to check the level of knowledge of letter names and letter sounds. These are the foundation of successful spelling and can be checked using the alphabet arc below.

You can create your own alphabet arc from plastic or wooden letters – a bag of 'Scrabble' letters works well. The advantage of using plastic letters are that it gives you flexible learning opportunities which will be explained later. I have been criticised for recommending Scrabble letters because they are presented in capital letters. While it is true that lower case letters are better, many households have a box of Scrabble making it easy to get started. If you are worried about using capital letters, then take a look at your computer keyboard, it is most likely in capitals and that doesn't stop children learning the different letters.

Letter names

Using the alphabet arc, or plastic letters, point to each letter in sequence and ask your child to tell you the *name* of each letter. Most children will be reasonably firm on the names of the letters in the alphabet. Then it is important to test 'automaticity', how automatically your child can link each letter to its name. The easiest way to do this is to point to letters at random and challenge your child to tell you the names. Use a pencil and point to various letters, moving to another as your child says the one you pointed to. Obviously it is important to build in success so do not move too quickly.

As a rule of thumb it is better to speed up gradually. If, in your estimation, your child is ready for a challenge, lay down an "I bet you can't" challenge, linked to a small reward (I am a firm believer in the power of small scale bribery and corruption based around smarties, etc.) and have some fun with it. Children often like to challenge us too – give it a go.

Letter sounds

This can be the tricky one. Now we are talking about the 'pure sound' that each letter makes. So the name of the letter 'a' becomes the 'ah' sound in 'cat', 'b' becomes the 'bu' sound in 'bird', etc. There are a number of websites which will give you pure sounds. Have a look at www.sparklebox.co.uk and www.genkienglish.net. This second site is for English as a second language and has many useful activities. The importance of parents modelling pure sounds cannot be over emphasised and it is important to guard against any tendencies to sound 'd' as 'dur', 'g' as 'ger', etc. Ask your children – they will know the pure sounds.

Using the same approach you used with letter names, work your way around the letters, this time asking for the sounds. When you are confident that the sounds are firm in the alphabetic sequence, point at random as before.

Filling in the gaps

If necessary, make a list of letter sounds which are not firm and practice them separately. You can make flash cards with pictures – preferably drawn by your child – or download from Sparklebox.

Smartkids (www.smartkids.co.uk) sell the Smart Chute which is well worth looking at for a range of learning activities.

Try concentrating on the problem letters/sounds and then putting them back into the alphabet arc.

It is quite likely that a child who lacks confidence in reading and/or spelling may not be automatic on letter sounds, in other words it may be necessary stop and think about certain sounds. Obviously this spoils the flow of any activity and can have a negative impact on the comprehension and fluency of reading and the organisation of ideas and spelling of words when writing. When your child is in this position it is important that you share this information with the school so that they can work with you to provide practice opportunities.

If, despite extra intervention in school, your child fails to pick up the sounds then this may be a problem which needs a school based investigation leading to resolution through a planned approach, perhaps a hearing test and maybe some small group support using a phonic programme.

Putting letter names and sounds together

Successful reading and spelling is more likely when children are completely automatic on names and sounds.

This is easily practised as follows by challenging your child to respond quickly and correctly when you:

1. Point to a letter and say 'name'
2. Point to another letter and say 'sound'

Do this randomly around the alphabet arc, speeding up and slowing down as appropriate. Remember the objective is success and fun, not to find another problem to fall out about. Make a note of any problem letters and sounds and work on them before putting them back and starting again. To experience just how tricky this activity can be, ask your child/your partner to test you and show no mercy!

Letters and sounds into spelling

Children who have reached the age of about 8 without 'catching' spelling run the risk of falling ever further behind. Assuming that letters and sounds are reasonably firm and accurate, even if not totally automatic (how automatic were you by the way?) the next step is to find ways of getting 'close enough' to the everyday jargon words that your child uses correctly in speech but struggles to spell.

The concept of 'close enough' is important, especially in the context of IT based spell checkers and, ultimately GCSEs. The spellchecker in Microsoft Word is very effective in suggesting a word that is reasonably close to the original, as is the superb handheld Franklin Spellcheck (available from most large electronic outlets). If, for example, you spell the word 'giraffe' as 'jiraf' (which is an appropriate phonic alternative because the letter combinations sound like the actual word) both spellcheckers give the correct spelling as one of a number of alternatives.

In GCSEs work is usually marked for content and then extra marks are awarded for spelling and grammar. Examiners will give credit for appropriate phonic alternatives as long as they are not a 'barrier to communication'. So writing "fotosinthesis" during a Biology exam conveys meaning and is acceptable because, knowing the context in which the word was used, we know what was intended.

Obviously the correct spelling is preferable but parents are urged to bear in mind that there are 'weak spellers' in university and industry who are successful because they can think, whereas accurate spellers with no ideas usually go nowhere fast.

In the right context and especially bearing in mind that at work so much is produced electronically and checked with a spellchecker, 'close enough is good enough'! So, while neat handwriting is still valued for esoteric reasons, I would say that every minute spent on handwriting practice needs to be matched with a minute spent learning to touch type.

In the real world, conveying information by handwriting is already more a matter of preference rather than necessity and, very soon, expressing that preference in the form of neat handwriting will be seen as 'quaint' rather than as the sign of being well educated. Many 'well-educated' people already use texts and e-mails via hand held devices for most purposes, including shopping lists and 'things to do'. My belief is that parental time is better spent developing touch typing and other related ICT skills, rather than worrying about handwriting skills.

Happy clappy spelling – a quick fix solution

Most children are able to say thousands of complicated words, usually a lot many more than they can comfortably spell. By using clapping appropriately, this gap between words they can say and words they can spell can be closed so the technique is the basis for a very effective approach to spelling. Happy clappy spelling can help minimise problems with letter names and letter sounds. It also fits well into the pragmatic 'close enough is good enough' philosophy which is a lifeline for so many highly intelligent children who, despite great teaching, just do not 'get' spelling and probably never will. Fortunately a word that is 'close enough' can easily be corrected via an electronic spellcheck, unfortunately traditional dictionaries are much less helpful, but more on dictionaries later.

The approach is based around syllables, which are the beats in a word. So 'piglet' has two syllables and 'photosynthesis' has five syllables. Put another way, and your child may well be able to help you here, you should be able to clap the syllable beats of all English words. It is easier to learn the five syllables or beats of pho/to/syn/the/sis rather than the 14 letters because the syllables give a 'big picture' structure which many children find fairly easy to remember.

The graphics below may help to make the point:

A word to the wise – note that 'kitten' is split as kit/ten. As a general principle it is essential that both 't' sounds are voiced. If split as kitt/en the child will only hear one 't' sound and, quite reasonably, go on to spell it kit/en.

Listen to the beats/claps of each word from the syllables. Sometimes it is necessary to stretch the pronunciation of a word to hear the syllables. Try saying a word like 'hospital' and stretch it so that each syllable beat become clear.

Another word to the wise – be careful with words like 'dragonfly' – it is best to split it as *drag*/on/fly rather that *dra*/gon/fly. In English the vowel at the end of a syllable usually says it's name rather than it's sound (think about mu/sic or sli/ding). So dra/gon/fly can actually sound like 'dray/gon/fly.

Here are some very basic rules and principles which will help parents to support their children with syllabification:

Rules and principles for splitting words into syllables

1. All syllables must contain a vowel, either a single vowel or a vowel combination (ai, ea, etc.). An exception word is 'rhythm' where 'y' acts as an 'occasional vowel'.

2. Always look to divide syllables between double consonants – bub/ble, hop/ping. If you do not such words often end up being spelt with only one vowel so bub/le becomes *buble* rather than bub/ble.

3. If there are more consonants try to separate a single consonant from the consonant blend – con/strict, trans/mu/ta/tion.

4. In a closed syllable, where the vowel is followed by a consonant, the vowel usually says its sound – tech/nol/o/gy, hos/pit/al.

5. In an open syllable, where the vowel is alone or at the end of the syllable, it usually says the vowel name – o/pen, e/mu, la/zy.

Make and Break - learning tricky words with the Mackay Method

Make and Break applies the same psychological principles to learning spellings as we used for learning the shopping list. In particular it builds in the important 'touchy/feely element' which is so important to learning for a majority of children, especially those who have struggled in the past.

Unlike 'Look-Cover-Write-Check', Make and Break harnesses a wide range of learning preferences, effectively allowing your child to personalise the process.

It works like this:

Using Make and Break to spell 'independent'

1. Using plastic letters, give your child the correct letters to spell the word.

2. Parental choice: either present the word spelt out in letters or present them in a jumble for your child to sort out.

3. Together, say the word and stretch it so that the syllables can be heard:
      innnnn/deeeee/pennnn/deeeeent.

4. Together 'clap and say' until the rhythm is right. Also try saying the word with a hand under the chin. It should be possible to 'feel' the syllables.

5. Ask "How many syllables have we got?" If the answer is not "4" we need to do it again.

6. If you have given your child the word in letters ask him/her to say "independent," physically split it into syllables and 'syllable speak' *in / de / pen / dent.*

7. If your child has the letters in a jumble, the task is to make the word, split it into syllables and then 'syllable speak' in/de/pen/dent.

8. Repeat these activities a number of times until firm.

9. Now jumble the letters again. The task now is to build the word saying the names of the letters as they are put in place: i-n-d-e-p-e-n-d-e-n-t.

10. Next split into syllables and syllable speak. Repeat steps 9 and 10 as often as necessary.

11. When you think the time is right (when you are pretty certain that success is very likely) ask your child to:
    a) Look at the word very carefully and 'take a photograph of it with your mind' (see the visualisation technique below)
    b) Cover the word
    c) Write it
    d) Check

Assuming success, we are now ready to learn another word.

This process is lengthy and time-consuming because it relies on the use of many learning preferences to ensure success, but as a result, the words are more likely to become lodged in the long term memory. It does get much quicker with practice, but it may require far too much time to learn a typical spelling list for the following week.

My advice is simple. Start by agreeing with the school that your child will only be learning half the words, or maybe 4 or 5 words, each week in order to use a strategy that, in the long term, will accelerate the learning process. Good schools will not have a problem with this, though individual teachers may lack the confidence to make an exception on behalf of one child. Once the issue has been discussed with the Head, the problem should go away. If it does not, in other words despite the Head saying only do half the spellings the teacher still expects them all, it will be necessary to go back to the Head once again. It can be very helpful to take another adult with you for this second meeting who can record what has been said and what has been agreed. The local Citizen's Advice Bureau will often find support for parents at these meetings and offer impartial advice and support.

Please do not assume this technique is only for younger children, I use it with `6th formers' who need to spell complex jargon words for A level subjects and also in my work with very well qualified dyslexic adults who need to spell certain words accurately.

Jargon Words

Geography	Environment
Technology	Application
Science	Volcanic
Photosynthesis	Eruption
Hypotenuse	Triangle
Multiplication	Difference

Working with "tricky words"

Around 80% of English words follow some sort of rule; it is the other 20% that cause the problem. Tricky words have unusual letter combinations and/or are hard to sound out in any logical way. One solution is to look for opportunities to say them as they are spelt.

So:

- 'Tuesday' becomes 'Tu/es/day'
- The same process gives us 'Wed/nes/day', 'Sci/ence', 'pe/op/le' etc.

For reasons which should be obvious, this strategy can only be used with words which are already part of your child's spoken vocabulary. Once you have established a form of syllable speak which works for a given word, use the plastic letters as before and go through the 'make and break' process.

Visualisation

Visualisation is about the ability to 'see' a word in the mind's eye, effectively developing a bank of sight words. These sight words form the basis of fluent reading and spelling.

Efficient readers use very little phonics in their reading; they tend to look at the first and last letter of a word and the shape and then use context and grammar to make an informed guess about pronunciation – "Today I will *read*; yesterday I *read.*" A similar approach is used by efficient spellers, they tend to write a word down to see if it 'looks right'. (See 'serial probability' below.)

Inviting your child to 'take a photograph with your mind' is very powerful and effective, though not all will find it the complete answer. I believe it is definitely worth trying to teach the skill of visualising words.

Choose a tricky word like *'because'*, *'said'*, etc. Then ask your child to:

1. "Photograph the word with your mind".

2. Next say "Close your eyes and try to see the word being written on your eyelids in bright red, fiery letters". Ask, "Can you see it?"

3. Then say "Open your eyes and project the word on to the wall, can you still see it?"

4. Finally say "Keep looking at it and tell me the letters you can see from right to left" – *esuaceb* etc. (the ability to do this proves that your child is actually 'seeing' the word on the wall - visualisation has occurred).

If successful ask your child to close the eyes again, visualise the word, open the eyes and write it. Not every child or adult will find this a natural strategy; but for those who do it can be very useful.

If your child is one of the lucky visualisers, point out how many words s/he can write on the eyelids and then take into a spelling test. As one of my students remarked, "Is that working smart or what?"

In reality this is a teachable skill and one worth persevering with, if only to support the necessary capacity to use sight words for reading and spelling.

Serial probability

This is a jargon way of asking the key question "What are the odds of certain letters going together?" A strong feel for serial probability enables children to proof read and make 'intelligent guesses' about:

i) Which letter combinations are probably needed to spell a given word?

ii) Which combinations that work phonetically and make the required sound but are not likely or probable?

For example, the sound 'shun' often occurs at the end of words and can be made in a number of ways. But it is very improbable in English for that sound to be spelt `shun'. On the other hand, it makes sense to spell the sound that way in terms of 'close enough spelling'. The most probable series of letters to get that sound in English are 'tion' followed by 'sion'.

Applying the principle of serial probability, a child who spells 'station' as 'stashun' needs to know how unlikely that letter combination is.

The bottom line with spelling comes back to the importance of conveying meaning. What parents and teachers must avoid is placing so much importance on correct spelling, especially by responding to errors with punitive approaches, like "write it out 10 times", that children stop trying to bring their rich spoken language into their writing and instead play safe. We want our children to risk writing "We enjoyed a superb holiday travelling through Andalucía" and not to decide to play it safe by writing "We went to Spain."

Pulling it all together

The best way to learn spellings is to use as many senses as possible and the use of plastic letters makes the process much easier. It is important to check sound symbol correspondence using the alphabet arc and practice weak letters. But it is also important to use the 'happy clappy' approach at the same time to support your child confidently to bring their spoken language closer to their written language.

Getting ideas down on paper

Homework tasks based around organising ideas into writing can be a nightmare and are often a perfect recipe for tears before bedtime. Most parents will know how frustrating it is to see our children staring at a blank piece of paper, getting more and more upset as we get more and more upset – the most vicious of vicious circles!

Quick fix

The quickest fix I know is to offer to be the scribe, the child talks and we write it down.

This approach has been very helpful in just getting 'something down' so we can all go to bed because these problems often rear their head at around 10.00pm on a Sunday night, having been put off until the last possible minute. If you do scribe it is important, as stated earlier, to play fair with the school and write down exactly what your child says, even if (or I would say especially if) it is completely wrong. Then send a note in with the homework explaining the situation.

However, this approach is no more than a temporary quick fix and it will not lay down the necessary foundations of good practice that your child will need in the future. In order to make the writing process more effective it is important that we understand what is going on in our child's head when s/he is trying to write.

It may be helpful to look at writing as information processing; basically information, ideas, etc. that are in the brain that need to be processed so they 'come out' as writing. The problem for many children is that their great ideas seem to get lost on the way to their pen, especially if there is undue emphasis on punctuation and spelling during the processing stage.

A 'stream of consciousness' approach can be very helpful here, especially if parents take on the role of secretary or scribe.

Too many ideas but cannot get started

An example of a 'can't get started' issue for many children is that they have plenty of ideas but they cannot get them in the right order. They are not natural 'beginning, middle, end' thinkers. In the long term their preferred eclectic style of thinking will prove very useful; they will become strategic thinkers who can predict, anticipate and respond without having to work through the straightjacket of linear thinking.

For the same reason, these children can find it difficult to plan their work, since many planning techniques assume that the starting point is known. So offer to scribe sentences or ideas on post-it notes as they talk. If you scribe in sentences, I suggest you leave a line between each sentence so you can cut them into strips for re-ordering if necessary.

Another 'starting issue' is having too many vivid ideas and not being able to select the best one. The limiting factor here is the frustration of starting to write and then having a change of mind and wasting all that writing. Again, the parent as scribe can take away the pressure of writing and allow or encourage as many false starts as are required.

A word to the wise – it has been known for children to manipulate the writing process by continually making false starts until, hopefully, the parents give up. In this scenario it is worth deciding on a finite number of false starts (three should be fine) and then choosing the best fit.

Always remember that, unless the homework is GCSE coursework, it only has to be good enough. This also enables us to support our children to make decisions about when to do 'a best job' and when an 'ok job' will do. Be prepared for some bad decisions in the early stages but this realistic and healthily cynical approach is important, especially for some, many, or maybe for all, homework tasks.

A staged approach to getting ideas down on paper

Stage 1 – Thinking without boundaries

The trick is to use a version of the tried and tested 'post-it' technique used during the paired reading exercise. With parents acting as scribes, the child thinks out loud and each point is written on a separate post-it and stuck randomly on the table. It is important that parents suspend all judgement during this process and basically stick to recording, unless an opportunity to add 'creative value' crops up.

Equally important is to acknowledge that this is no more than an initial brainstorming process which will require the ideas to be filtered as the next stage. At the end of a brainstorm the table should look can look like this.

Structuring the thinking

Although a 'stream of consciousness' has its place, it may be helpful to provide a structure or framework to organise the ideas, your child will be familiar with this approach in school. A simple framework is to ask "First, Next, After that, Then, Also, Finally," etc. Another is the simple "Beginning, Middle, End". See Section 2, page 88 for examples of organising mind maps.

Often the thinking can be chunked quite naturally by the nature of the task. For example, the assignment: *"What causes global warming? Explain the impact on low lying islands. What do you think we should do next?"* requires three separate brain-storming sessions, one for each part of the task. My preference is to work on one chunk at a time and process it all the way though, as described below, before starting on the next one.

Stage 2 – Select and order

I value all ideas during Stage 1, but clearly some ideas will be more valuable than others. Taking the global warming assignment as an example, the first chunk will have plenty of 'post-it ideas' on causation; some are wonderful, others are typical and some are irrelevant - that is the random nature of effective thinking. Now we need to select in order to build a framework for paragraph 1.

I tend to ask my students to 'go for 5' and encourage them to select the five most interesting and appropriate ideas and stick them on the table in the best order in which to use them. Five seems to be a magic number of Ideas in a paragraph but it is only a guide. If you have more than five ideas, stick the spare ones to one side, they may well be useful later.

Stage 3 – The Plan

Earlier I made the point that many bright children find it hard to plan because they have too many ideas in their heads. By Stage 3 the ideas are not only out of their heads, but are also on post-it notes so they are touchable and moveable.

As we found with the learning and spelling activities, 'touchy/feely' is essential and effective for a majority of children of all ages. In fact, the older the learner, the more important it is to keep the hands-on approaches.

Now we need a personalized structure on which to hang the ideas. It could look like this:

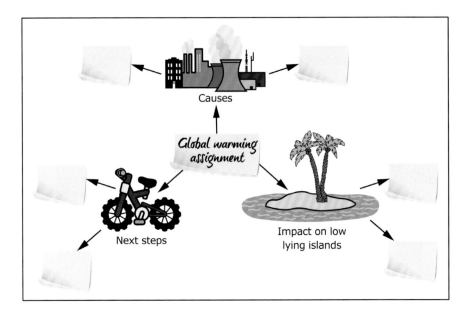

More linear thinkers may prefer this using the software program, *Inspiration*:

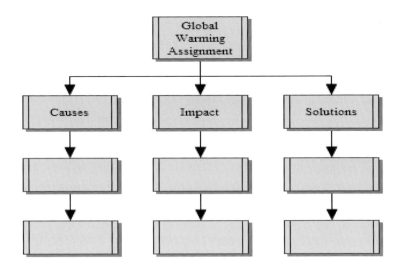

Older children may prefer a different version of this model (also from *Inspiration*):

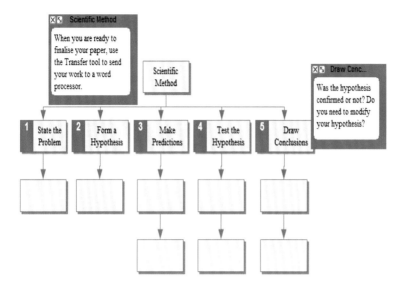

I. State the Problem

Regardless of the complexity of the problem work to reduce it to a simple statement.

A. *"The job is to explain global warming and solve the problem of low lying islands."*

II. Form a Hypothesis

Propose a theory based on information you have gathered or what you have observed.

A. _____

_____

III. Make Predictions

What would happen if your hypothesis were true? How can your hypothesis be tested?

A. _____

B. _____

IV. Test the Hypothesis

Design an experiment to test the hypothesis. Be sure to record your experimental procedure and observations.

A. _____

B. _____

V. Draw Conclusions

Was the hypothesis confirmed or not?

Do you need to modify your hypothesis?

A. _____

B. _____

A less structured approach is:

In every case I advise parents to offer a range of templates, allowing the child to choose. Then support your child to stick the post-it notes on to the plan to create a flow of ideas, linking each note with a short line.

Stage 4 - Modifying and improving

At this stage some of the rejected ideas may come into play as thinking develops. Because we are using a hands-on approach there is no problem to swapping some notes or changing the order of others and this is one of the strengths of this strategy: it is never finished until it is finished.

This flexibility really appeals to many children, especially those who hate messy work and prefer to screw it up and start again. Now all they have to do is 'unstick and move', which is much more efficient.

Stage 5 - Improving and enhancing

It may be that fresh ideas are generated during the modifying process. If they are, either write them directly onto the plan or, much preferred, write them onto post-it notes and get your child to stick them in the appropriate place and link with a line.

Stage 6 - Talking into writing

Having got to this stage it is a great temptation to say, "Now write it up". While some children may be ready to do so, most benefit from this next step, which is arguably the jewel in the crown of the process. Your child now needs to use the plan to tell you the story that is outlined in the post-it notes. It usually helps if parents give a sentence to get the paragraph started, for example:

"There are many reasons for global warming. Some people say...."

Something as simple as this is all it usually takes to get your child into the flow. I suggest you ask your child to work around the plan, pointing to each post-it and explaining what it means, all the time encouraging him/her to add any extra detail that may occur to them. As they are talking, the parent needs to be writing down exactly what is said, warts and all, as the first draft. What usually happens is that each post-it note become several sentences as one idea triggers another.

Stage 7 - Writing into talking

When you have transcribed one paragraph, stop and pair read the work so far. This is an opportunity for your child to hear what has been written and it is usually a time for celebration. It is also the time for some editing, below are a number of editing principles which will add value to a paragraph.

Please do not try to use them all at once; instead drip feed them at appropriate moments over the coming weeks and months.

- Only one 'and' in a sentence. Not a firm rule but a good starting point for controlling the 'and then' tendency. Once 'and' is under control of course it can be used more than once.

- Consecutive sentences must never begin with the same word. This is a firm rule. The 'First, Next, After that' plan will help within paragraphs as well as for actual paragraph starters.

- Find a noun (A 'naming word'. At its most simple, a noun is something you can take a photograph of). Ask, "Can you add a great adjective (describing word) to tell me more about the noun?" Do the same with verbs and adverbs.

For example:

> *"The fumes from factories raise carbon dioxide levels in the atmosphere...."*

can become:

> *"<u>Poisonous</u> fumes from <u>polluting</u> factories raise..."*

Try starting a sentence with a word that ends in 'ing' or 'ly':

> *"Thinking about the problem..."* or
> *"Surprisingly..."*

Despite an often blanket ban in school, feel free to begin sentences with *'because'*, but only if your child knows how to do it. *'Because'* as a sentence starter is useful for cause and effect:

> *"Because of global warming a number of experts say..."*

Now repeat the process for paragraphs 2 and 3 until the assignment is completed. The version in parental handwriting is the one that goes back to school, unless your child wishes to have a go. In that case I strongly suggest you hide the copy you have just made – if you do not your child will end up making a best copy which is a total waste of time. On the other hand, a different copy, perhaps with different mistakes, can be a thing of added value. Please do not make the common mistake of confusing neatness with value.

Planning with mind maps

Sometimes called concept maps or spider diagrams, the principles are fundamentally the same. The beauty of this way of planning is that it does not require your child to begin at the beginning, the map develops organically and, once finished, a starting point can be selected. (See also page 88, in section 2.)

Managing behaviour for learning

Most parents have experienced the stress of trying to manage 'behaviour for learning'; supporting our children to develop the life skills of positive, 'can do' approaches to work, resilience in the face of difficulty, and recognising that 'when the going gets tough...'. One of the problems is that our bright, perceptive and often very manipulative children have learnt 'behaviour to avoid learning' and they are experts in deploying these skills.

A typical scenario could be:

> Parent: "Time for homework."
> Child: "I hate you and I hate my homework."
> Parent: "Don't you talk to me like that. Go to your room!"

So now the child has avoided the homework and is very happy in the bedroom with his/her TV, Wii, Facebook, etc. There is little doubt who came out on top in that little conflict!

Examining the psychology of persuasion may be helpful in developing the good habits of managing behaviour for learning. First it is important to establish a basic principle which I was very slow to realise as a parent myself. It is summed up in the picture and caption below:

This is a picture of my dog, Patch, a very manipulative spaniel, who quickly worked out that looking cute with a lead in his mouth leads to 'walkies'. Working with Patch has led me to develop a whole new way of thinking about managing the behaviour of children because, as a bottom line, Patch will only do what I want him to do if *he* wants to do it – does that sound like our children? In other words, to get Patch to behave, the 'wiifme' factor (what's in it for me) must be suitably high, without going over the top.

Harsh but true

Applying the 'wiifme' principle to homework needs careful and sensitive handling. Wholesale bribery and corruption is unsustainable and gives the wrong message to our children. On the other hand, appealing to 'divine self-interest' is also very powerful so, as another bottom line, it is important to appreciate that parents must not care more about homework than their children. Put crudely, the consequences of a failure to complete homework will be on the shoulders of the children rather than the parents. Never lose sight of that important reality, which is harsh but true.

On the other hand, no one wants a child to be upset, stressed and unhappy, especially when that child is trying really hard, but is perhaps working hard rather than smart. So managing behaviour for learning perhaps operates at two levels.

Managing your child to:

1. Work in effective personalised ways which may initially take a bit more effort (basically being prepared to change the inefficient work habits of a lifetime)

2. Eliminate the well established, tried, tested and very effective diversionary tactics designed to avoid settling down to work; this is sometimes known as 'SNOT' – secondary, non obvious tantrums, of which more later.

Working Smart not Hard

The techniques and strategies that form the body of this book (summarised in Section 2) are simple and personalised ways to support your child to work more quickly and effectively. But they need to be practiced and we need to pay our children the compliment of persistence – taught is not learnt. Some of the techniques will need a great deal of reinforcement if they are to replace the "comfort zone" approaches which are familiar and secure, even though often a complete waste of time.

Sadly, though typically, it is often the brighter children who are most reluctant to embrace new ways of working. They will acknowledge that their way may not be very efficient, but they cling on to it because, *"It is my way and you said I can do it the way I think best!"*; and they will argue convincingly for their way!

An effective response is to stand firm and make your offer of support conditional on working 'smart', that is to say using the personalised techniques that have already been proven to work. Then your child has a safe choice to make – work alone or work with support – and it is important that we make a low key/zero emotion withdrawal from the situation while always leaving the door open for support. This works for me:

"Ok, you do it your way. I think that we have been more successful working the other way but it is up to you. If you change your mind I will be ...."

A cautionary tale

Put a time limit on how long you are prepared to be available, especially if working in the evening.

My daughter realised that asking for help at 9.30 at night would elicit a really quick and positive response in order to get everything finished in time for bed. When this became part of a manipulative strategy we laid down a ground rule which was that any homework tasks not mentioned before 7.00 p.m. were not supported – she was on her own.

Like most loved children my daughter did not believe that her father could be so mean and, one Sunday night at about 9.30 p.m., she came down with a pile of homework to be completed by Monday. I stood firm – it was horrible; she went to bed in tears, then got into trouble in school the next day and, but for most of her remaining time in school and later in college, she followed the ground rule.

This was a classic bit of 'cruel to be kind' parenting and when, on the odd occasion, she did genuinely forget something, I was only too willing to help out. Was I being manipulated? Probably I was, but an important part of being a parent, is knowing when to standing firm and then being manipulated with your eyes open.

As a rule of thumb, the more thoroughly I have practiced learning strategies for reading, spelling, writing etc, the more willing my children have been to use them. The strategies need to be practiced to mastery and re-visited regularly to make sure they are still working. If not, they need to be 're-personalised' and tweaked according to developing preferences; by this I mean an early preference for, say, mind mapping, may be replaced by flow charts, so time spent re-visiting some linear sequential planning techniques will be a worthwhile investment.

Avoiding S.N.O.T.

The 'secondary, non obvious tantrum' is a well used strategy for avoiding something which is proving difficult. It works like this: the parent asks a low key question about a routine responsibility – it could be as simple as "don't forget it is your turn to clear the table/load the dishwasher, etc". The child over reacts, becomes rude and behaves in an unacceptable way, leaving the parents with little apparent option but to send the child to bed. This, of course, was what the tantrum was intended to achieve, now the table will be cleared by someone else.

The problem here is that we parents tend to 'bite' on the secondary behaviour, the language, the attitude, etc. and so lose sight of the original focus, in this case to get the table cleared. In this scenario the SNOT has won the day.

Suppose instead we had the confidence to ignore the SNOT and focus on getting a result. At its simplest the exchange could go like this:

Parent: "Time for you to clear the table / stack the dishwasher / go and do your homework".

Your child over reacts with SNOT: "I hate you, you're always picking on me, etc.",

This you completely ignore. Instead you take a deep breath and say something like "I'm sorry you feel that way. Get it done and we can talk about it."

Then you might need to use a well tried technique: 'the broken record'.

The broken record

The broken record is a simple way for parents to stand their ground and emphasise what is required without getting angry.

It works best when we make a statement of need, preferably beginning with the word 'I' (more about the importance of 'I' statements" later) and keep repeating it without looking angry, raising the voice etc. A broken record response to the scenario above could be: "I need you to clear the table, then we can talk about it."

There are two key ground rules:

1. **No further explanation is given** – just keep repeating the statement of need

2. **Do not get drawn into arguments** – because, when the tantrum fails to get the desired result, the next phase of the encounter will be to start a row, gradually upping the ante in order to get sent to bed in time for the next episode of.....

Making 'I' Statements

Two killer phrases in any relationship are "You always" and "You never". Another one guaranteed to wind up any child (and quite rightly) is a version of "Why can't you be more like...." That is just asking for SNOT.

"I feel" statements enable us to express anger, frustration, whatever, in assertive and effective ways which are much less personal that "You always".

These statements give a clear indication of our perception of the problem and how it can be addressed.

To continue with the dishwasher scenario:

"I need you to stack the dish washer" is the 'assertive I' statement of need which may well be the best broken record response as well. Be prepared to allow some thinking time, teachers often call it 'take up time'. An angry child who is being thwarted and then manipulated and who realises that the only way out is to do what is asked, often needs to save face by responding slowly. The message s/he is trying to communicate is, "I could defy you if I wanted to but this time, as a big favour, I'll do what you want". Giving take up time gives the child a chance to make a gesture and then get on with it.

Giving take up time

Another word to the wise - do not stare at your child or point your finger during take up time, this risks undoing all the previous good work as the child may take exception and decide that more SNOT may actually carry the day; time is passing and s/he is beginning to feel that life as we know it will collapse unless MSN is accessed immediately.

Making the statement of need and then talking to someone else in a really normal, cool and relaxed tone of voice actually communicates the total expectation that what has been asked for will be done – eventually.

Then it becomes a battle of wills, basically who can 'out ignore' who for the longest. This is one game that we parents need to win.

The bottom line is that it does not matter how long it takes as long as, eventually, 'it' is done. Compromise is good, try a version of, "I can see you are desperate to go on Facebook. If I do your chores now, what will you do for me tomorrow when I ask you to do something? Is that a deal?"

Going for 'win, win'

A 'win-win' situation is very simple – both parties get some, or perhaps even all, of the result they are looking for. Making it work depends on the adult being an adult and being prepared to 'tactically ignore' SNOT and 'outwait' the other protagonist, maybe even choosing to step back, in favour of longer term results down the line.

Watch out for your child trying to out score you. A typical response to a request to tidy up might be, paradoxically, "But I was just going to do my homework". Once again, be the adult, be in control and decide which result is the most appropriate. Sometimes it will be deferring chores in favour of homework and sometimes chores must come first, especially if homework has been in the frame for hours but has not been completed because of urgent MSN commitments. In either scenario a useful pattern of words is something like this:

"Of course you can do .... as soon as you've done...."

If you feel the situation merits it, offer to help.

"I'll tell you what, you take the plates out and I'll load the dishwasher. That way you can get onto your homework sooner." This works for doing homework first before sorting out the social life. Or, "Of course you can go on Facebook – just as soon as you've done your homework."

Alternatively, would it help if:

- You told me what to write and I write it down?
- We do a TCP-QR together and then pair read the passage?
- You tell me some ideas and I'll put them on post-it notes?

Don't get mad, just get even

Whatever the outcome, there is the significant matter of inappropriate behaviour which must be addressed at some time in the near future.

Most families will have some rules about behaviour, often unvoiced but they are there none the less. They are often versions of, "It's ok to be angry but:

- Don't hurt others – especially the ones you love and who love you
- Don't hurt yourself or threaten to do so – self harming is often the sign of a much deeper rooted problem, the threat is usually more about attempting to control the current situation
- Don't damage property – trashing a bedroom means two chores – making good plus the original task."

Unacceptable behaviour can be tactically ignored as long as it does not put others at risk and especially if ignoring it means that we as parents get a result. But there must always, always be a reckoning and it is important that your child knows this to be the case and actually expects it to happen.

The trick is to wait until the situation has calmed down and then using phrases like "I feel....... when you........" and then begin to unpack the behaviour and rebuild the relationship.

This approach will be effective for parents in role as parents, (basically in role as the mature and responsible adult in the relationship who will make and take hard decisions if necessary).

It will be much less effective, possibly totally ineffective, for parents in role as 'best friend'. Best friends can take the short term view and go for easy solutions. Parents recognise that tough love is the answer and like and respect their children too much to accept potentially damaging behaviour.

I do appreciate how hard it can be to dig in and stand up for important principles like "We agreed that you would do your homework at this time", especially when our children are ruthlessly pushing every emotional button they can reach.

But it is important to know when to give a little and when to stand firm; the long term benefits of being the responsible adult are immeasurable, no matter how apparently distressing they may be at the time. Bear in mind also that, being human, we parents will get it wrong from time to time; but we will not get it wrong as often as parents who negate their responsibilities as adults and try to be best friends with the complex bundle of emotions that is their child.

SECTION 2

Core Learning Strategy

Learning Preference	Learning Technique
1.	
2.	
3.	

Each time I learn I will make sure I:

1. ....

2. ....

3. ....

Getting ideas down on paper:
Mind maps to copy

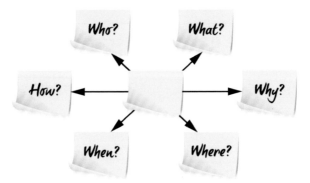

This model works well with paired reading. Children stop when they find a 'who' or a 'what' etc. and highlight the relevant information. I suggest you copy or reproduce the mind map onto a large sheet of paper (A3 or bigger). The highlighted information is then transferred to post-it notes – one piece of information per post-it – and stuck onto the mind map.

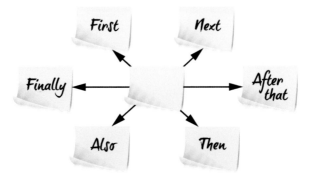

This model is most successful when trying to organise ideas into a logical order. It works best when children have an idea of what they want to write and are encouraged to shout out their ideas as they occur while the adult writes them down on separate post-it notes. The post-it notes can then be organised into a logical order once the idea generating process has finished.

Learning how to learn: the Police kit list

In Section 1, I showed how easy is can be to learn information which is presented as a list. The following two activities offer you the opportunity to practice learning lists before applying the principles to creating more learnable lists from typical homework tasks.

Below is another 'learnable list'. Let's apply the principles we used to learn the shopping list to this task:

1. All items written on separate post-it notes. Invite your child to illustrate the items on each post-it.

Below is a list of equipment usually carried/worn by a police officer. You have 15 minutes to organize the information and learn it for a test

- Radio pouch
- Chemical spray
- Handcuffs
- Whistle
- Knife
- Flashlight
- Safety boots
- Baton
- Key holder
- Gloves
- First aid kit
- Radio
- Notebook
- Body armour
- Reflective jacket

---

2. Support your child to come up with a set of organising headings under which the items can be grouped for example, safety, communication etc. Write each heading on a post-it note and organise the items as in the box below. Ideally each heading should have a maximum of 4-5 items to avoid overloading the memory.

> Start by organizing the information into groups which make sense to you.
>
> · For example:
>
> · <u>Clothing</u>:
>   Gloves
>   Reflective jacket
>   Safety boots
>
> · <u>Communication</u>
>   ??????
>   ??????
>   ?????

3. You have now created a form of flow chart with the items of kit organised in a way which makes sense to your child and the recall process has already started in the brain. But doing anything once is not enough to secure long term recall, brains need to process information in different ways if the information is to get into the long term memory.

4. Change the flow chart into either a mind map or a labelled diagram – no need to re-write the notes, just take them from the flow chart and reorganise.

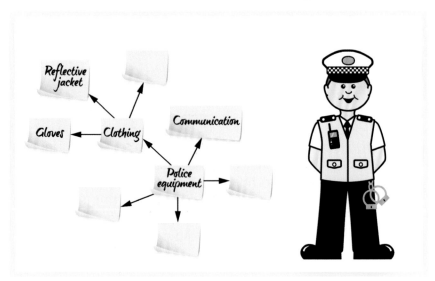

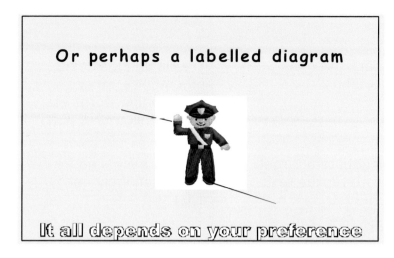

Or perhaps a labelled diagram

It all depends on your preference

5. In the spirit of working smart rather than hard, the final challenge (before the 'kit list test') is to come up with a way of learning the headings – Buzan's 'basic ordering ideas'. So if, for example, the basic ordering ideas are 'safety', 'communication', 'protection', and 'clothing', your child needs to come up with a preferred way of learning those key words.

How to learn a list – summary table	
Write each bit of information on a post-it note	Best if parents write and children illustrate
Organise under suitable headings	Try to limit the number of post-its to 4-5 per heading
Create a flow chart	Stick post-its under each heading, adjust as appropriate
Transform the flow chart	Use the post-its to create a mind map or labelled diagram

Learn the main headings	Try clapping, singing, mnemonics, story using the heading words etc. This is the critical part.
Negotiate a target score for the test	Make it easy – go for 8/15, definitely not 15/15!
Time to test	Ask your child to tell you the headings
Child to create the flow chart, mind map etc	Just start with the main headings
List the kit items that are associated with each heading	If s/he gets stuck try saying, "Close your eyes, can you see your picture/mind map?"
Mark it together	Be proud!

When your child can do this s/he is ready for the final part of the Kit List Challenge which is to:

Write down the headings from memory and:

Either: List the items of kit under each heading

Or: Use the headings to reproduce the mind map/labelled diagram and list the kit items in this way

A word to the wise -
(1) You will have realised by now that the only conscious 'learning' that took place was to do with the four or five headings. The actual list was learnt almost accidentally, basically by 'doing' it with the post-its, the mind maps etc.

So you can imagine how powerful this technique becomes when time is actually invested in learning the separate items as well. But the key is always to chunk under appropriate headings and learn the headings first.

(2) The success of this approach depends on very relaxed parenting and supporting children to set realistic targets. Be very careful about stress levels – stress destroys memory! Also please ensure early success by giving clues and hints as necessary.

Using Paired Reading to create 'learnable lists'

Decide what you need to find in the passage	Have highlighters ready
Decide if you need to look for any themes	For example you might consider different colours for a 'who, what, why, where, when, how,' analysis
Pair read and encourage your child to stop when information is spotted.	If your child misses important points try stopping yourself and ask if there is anything we need to highlight
Highlight as few words a possible	Less is definitely more, more words means more learning – definitely not smart!

Using TCP-QR for comprehension homeworks

The passage that follows is a typical homework. The task is to answer the questions in Part A but we are going to do it the smart way, using TCP–QR.

Title – What can we get from Venus ?
This is about getting the big picture and establishing context which will help with reading fluency when we come to pair reading the passage.

If this was a genuine homework task it is likely that your child will already have some knowledge about the subject. In this case I would ask for any prior knowledge about the planet, just to get the task started.

Captions and pictures
This is about beginning to chunk down to some of the detail. It also supports the build up of contextual knowledge which will allow intelligent guesses on unfamiliar words.

Look at the first two pages. Support your child with the reading of the paragraph headings, looking at the pictures and captions and also the data in the box.

Try asking "What have we found out so far?" I would expect us to have found out that:

- Venus might be the twin of earth
- It is permanently covered in clouds; and I'd be asking why that might be a problem for scientists?
- It is the second planet from the sun so what might the climate be like?

and so on.

During this process words in the passage will often 'leap out' at the reader, encourage reading of these but try to discourage reading big chunks of prose. However, reading short phrases may be very helpful at this point.

Questions (1) - Pair read the questions

As you go through the questions, ask if any answers are known already and make a note as you go. Some of the likely answers may prove to be wrong once you start to read the passage, but for now the answers are valid in terms of current knowledge of the passage.
I would expect many children to be able to answer Questions 4, 5 and 7 as a minimum before needing to read the passage.

Questions (2) – skimming and scanning for answers using target and trigger words (This is where it can get tricky!)

Let's start with an easy one: "What did Mariner 5 show Venus was really like?" The best target word is probably 'Mariner 5', so we skim and scan for it. When it is found we 'read around it' to see if the answer is there.

Ask your child to skim for the word and then be ready to pair read the sentence to see if it gives the answer. Then try Question 4 – target words being `main features', and so on.

Be careful with Question 1 – there are two possible target words, `Mariner 5' and `scientists'. You need to find and read around both words in order to get to the right answer. You have been warned!

Reading – time for paired reading

Now pair read the passage in order to:

1. Check the accuracy of the answers so far and modify as appropriate.

2. See if you can answer any questions that did not respond to the TCP-QR process.

How many questions can you answer before you read the passage on the following pages?

1. What did scientists think Venus was like before the Mariner 5 probe?

2. What were their reasons for believing this?

3. What did Mariner 5 show Venus was really like?

4. Why is Venus not a "promising destination" for a manned landing?

5. What are the main features of the surface of the planet?

6. What is interesting about these main features of the planet?

7. Why is it a waste of time looking at Venus through a telescope?

VENUS

Venus – Earth's Twin?

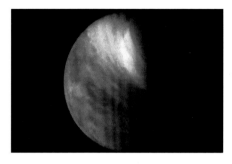 Venus is the second planet from the sun. It was once thought to be a twin of the earth because it is the closest of the other planets to Earth. The thick cloudy atmosphere led scientists to consider Venus to be very much like Earth during the Carboniferous era. The scientists imagined Venus to be covered with dense rain forests and amphibians, reptiles and maybe even dinosaurs.

When the unmanned space probe, Mariner 5, reached Venus it showed it to be a `pressure cooker planet' which was smothered in clouds of sulphuric acid. These clouds whirl around the planet giving it the distinctive v-shaped patterns that people associate with Venus. One effect of the thick clouds is that so much heat is retained that the temperature at the surface is hot enough to melt lead.

Instead of being a planet like Earth, Venus is a very hostile place which can burn visitors to a cinder, crush them flat and then dissolve them in sulphuric acid. So Venus is very different, very dangerous and a very unpromising destination for a manned space flight.

The Landscape

American and Russian probes have penetrated the dense acidic clouds, and mapped the surface of the planet.

The main features are two huge upland continents, though they are not surrounded by water as on Earth. They are called Ishtar Terra and Aphrodite Terra. These unusual names are interesting because they are the names of love goddesses from different cultures.

Venus is the second planet from the sun

Our Solar System

Searching for Venus

Venus is the brightest object in the sky, after the sun and the moon, and so it is one of the easiest planets to find. When the conditions are right Venus shines so brightly it can actually cast a shadow. But, because of the thick clouds of sulphuric acid there is not much to see when looking at Venus through a telescope.

Earth during the Carboniferous period

Venus in numbers

Diameter	12,104 km
Average Distance from Sun	108.2 million km
Mass	4.87×10^{24} kg
Size compared to Earth	0.95x
Gravity compared to Earth	0.88x
Surface Temperature	484°C (730K)
Length of day	243 Earth days (retrograde)
Length of year	224.7 days
Eccentricity of Orbit	0.00677
Density	5.25g/cm^3
Atmosphere	Carbon Dioxide - 96%
	Nitrogen - 3.5%
	Sulphur Dioxide, Argon and
	Carbon Monoxide - 0.5%